WHAT CAN WE DO?

POVERTY AND FOOD

KATIE DICKER

T0395610

Cavendish Square

Published in 2025 by Cavendish Square Publishing, LLC
2544 Clinton Street, Buffalo, NY 14224

First published in Great Britain in 2023 by Hodder & Stoughton
Copyright © Hodder & Stoughton, 2023

Website: cavendishsq.com

This publication represents the opinions and views of the author based on his or her personal experience, knowledge, and research. The information in this book serves as a general guide only. The author and publisher have used their best efforts in preparing this book and disclaim liability rising directly or indirectly from the use and application of this book.

The website addresses (URLs) included in this book were valid at the time of going to press. However, it is possible that contents or addresses may have changed since the publication of this book. No responsibility for any such changes can be accepted by either the author or the publisher.

Editor: Katie Dicker
Designer: Clare Nicholas
Series Designer: Dan Prescott

Picture acknowledgements:
Shutterstock: oticki cover t, Tinnakorn Jorruang cover b, Riccardo Mayer 4, spixel 5, Ivan Vasylyev 6, Talukdar David 7, Denys Kurbatov 8, Pavlo Baliukh 9, Scott Book 10, artichoke studio 11, BearFotos 12, Mr. Amarin Jitnathum 13, Elena Dijour 14, FOTOGRIN 16, Amors photos 17b, Kelvin H. Haboski 19, Andrei Armiagov 20, Alena Haurylik 22, Karol Moraes 23, Alex Segre 24, Es sarawuth 25t, Theerasak Namkampa 25b, Sergey Kohl 28; Getty: Westend61 15; Alamy: REUTERS 17t, 18, 21, Islandstock 26, ARCTIC IMAGES 27, Jake Lyell 29.

All design elements from Shutterstock.

Every attempt has been made to clear copyright. Should there be any inadvertent omission, please apply to the publisher for rectification.

Cataloging-in-Publication Data

Names: Dicker, Katie.
Title: Poverty and food / Katie Dicker.
Description: Buffalo, NY : Cavendish Square Publishing, 2025. | Series: What can we do? | Includes glossary and index.
Identifiers: ISBN 9781502673886 (pbk.) | ISBN 9781502673893 (library bound) | ISBN 9781502673909 (ebook)
Subjects: LCSH: Poverty--Juvenile literature. | Food security--Juvenile literature.
Classification: LCC D53 2025 | DDC --dc23

CPSIA compliance information: Batch #CW25CSQ: For further information contact Cavendish Square Publishing LLC at 1-877-980-4450.

Printed in the United States of America

Find us on

CONTENTS

WHAT IS POVERTY?

When someone lives in poverty, they are poor. They have few possessions and a low income. Some people live in extreme poverty – they can't meet their basic everyday needs such as food, shelter, heating, and clothing. Poverty can also mean not being able to access essential services, such as education, healthcare, sanitation, and electricity.

Where in the world?

Poverty occurs in all countries but is most common in sub-Saharan Africa and South Asia. More recently, conflict has caused poverty to rise in Northern Africa and the Middle East too. In 2022, World Bank figures showed that around 10 percent of the world's population live in extreme poverty, on less than US$2.15 a day – known as the "international poverty line." Sub-Saharan Africa is currently the world's poorest region, where over 40 percent of people live in extreme poverty.

This girl is collecting drinking water in sub-Saharan Africa. The long walk means there's little time left for education.

Relative poverty

Countries are classified as high-, middle-, or low-income, depending on their wealth and the size of their population. Because the cost of living differs between nations, wealthier countries are assessed with a higher "poverty line" figure. When someone is unable to meet their everyday needs, we call it "absolute poverty." But we also talk about "relative poverty" – the income needed to maintain an average standard of living in a particular place.

In high-income countries, poverty can mean not being able to join in with everyday activities and perhaps facing discrimination because of your financial situation or other circumstances.

Call for action

In 2015, the United Nations (UN) set a series of "sustainable development goals," aiming to end all poverty and hunger by 2030. These were ambitious targets, but extreme poverty had been falling for 25 years so it was worth striving for. But times change. Conflict, climate change, and the Covid-19 pandemic have now presented us with additional challenges. In this book, we will look at the causes of poverty and food insecurity, their impact on people and places, and what we can do to help resolve them.

IT'S A FACT

In 1990, 36 percent of the world's population lived in extreme poverty. By 2015, this figure had decreased to 10 percent, partly due to the effects of globalization and economic growth.

WHAT CAUSES POVERTY?

There is no single cause of poverty. Instead, a variety of factors can affect a person's access to everyday needs. To have a stable income, you need a steady job (and the skills or education to acquire it) but external factors can get in the way, and these may be beyond your control.

Difficult circumstances

Sometimes it can be difficult to get a job – there are more jobs in cities, for example, than in rural areas. A country may be facing a recession (an economic decline) with fewer jobs available, or ill health may prevent a person from working.

In extreme cases, conflict or disasters can disrupt jobs, education, and the economy. When Russia invaded Ukraine in 2022, for example, many Ukrainian companies closed or reduced their workforce, and unemployment almost doubled.

This abandoned glass factory was partially destroyed during the Russian invasion of Ukraine in 2022. Nearly five million jobs were lost in Ukraine during the first months of the conflict.

Additional struggles

In some parts of the world, people face discrimination because of their race, religion, or gender, making it more difficult to access education or job opportunities. Transportation may be too expensive to attend a school or workplace, or road infrastructure may be lacking. Internet access can also be limited, making it difficult to get information or to connect with others. Sometimes, extreme circumstances have a wide-reaching effect. The Covid-19 pandemic, for example, disrupted many jobs and sources of income, affecting both rich and poor.

Global support

In 1944, towards the end of the Second World War (1939–1945), the World Bank and the International Monetary Fund (IMF) were created to reduce poverty and to stabilize the global economy. The World Bank continues to offer loans or grants to help countries develop, while the IMF keeps track of the global economy and helps countries in crisis.

These children are being taught at a makeshift school under a railway bridge in New Delhi, India. Poverty means that over 30 million children in India have never been to an official school.

IT'S A FACT

In response to the Covid-19 pandemic, the World Bank provided over US$157 billion to help lower-income countries cope with and recover from the crisis.

RISING PRICES

The "cost of living crisis" is a news headline we have all come to recognize. Prices can rise around the world when conditions change, making a difficult situation much worse for those already struggling. Disruption to supply chains, higher demand for certain goods, and the effects of conflict, climate change, or disasters can cause the price of some goods to rocket.

Knock-on effect

When the price of crude oil goes up, fuel and fertilizers increase in cost too, making transportation, heating, and farming more expensive. In 2022, the Russian invasion of Ukraine affected oil prices because oil imports from Russia were restricted. Farmers needed fuel for their tractors and fertilizers for their crops, as well as feed for their animals. When conflict and extreme weather disrupt food supplies, a high demand for fewer goods makes things even more expensive.

Our food bills are rising. Many staple foods, such as milk and potatoes, have seen a sharp increase in price due to disrupted supplies and higher energy costs.

Price shocks

Some countries are particularly vulnerable to price increases because they only rely on a few nations for their supplies. Lebanon, for example, relies heavily on Russia and Ukraine for food imports such as wheat and sunflower oil. When the Russia-Ukraine war disrupted supplies, the price of these imports increased dramatically. To avoid price shocks in the future, countries need to become more self-sufficient or to import their supplies from a variety of nations.

KEEPING TRADE MOVING

With its rich, fertile soil, Ukraine is one of the most farmed countries in the world, and its ports on the Black Sea are good for exports. At the start of the Russia-Ukraine war, millions of tons of grain was trapped in Ukraine because ports were closed and transportation was restricted. Thankfully, international negotiations secured a deal to resume exports, guiding cargo ships safely through mined areas and helping to stabilize price increases.

These are wheat storage tanks in Ukraine. In times of peace, this country is a key exporter of wheat, barley, corn, and sunflower oil.

WHAT IS FOOD INSECURITY?

Every day, over 800 million people go to bed hungry and 50 million people face famine. Another two billion people experience food insecurity. This is when they have unreliable access to affordable, nutritious food. And despite our ability to make more food than ever before, these statistics have more than doubled in recent years.

Where are we now?

Food insecurity can start when there are threats to its availability, accessibility, and affordability. We currently produce enough food for everyone, but too much food is wasted, and poverty and inequality restrict access. Crop yields and supplies can be disrupted by climate change, conflict, and natural disasters, and price increases can make fresh nutritious food unaffordable. With a rising population, we need to keep food supplies sustainable and tackle causes of hunger and food insecurity.

Drought conditions have caused this corn crop to fail. The UN estimates that by 2050, droughts may affect over three-quarters of the world's population.

Disabled people have an increased risk of food insecurity due to restricted opportunities and income. About 15 percent of the world's population lives with some form of disability.

Restricted access

Food insecurity affects people with low incomes, but also people who have difficulty shopping for food – perhaps because they're unwell or they have no transportation. War and conflict can disrupt supplies, leaving some supermarket shelves empty. Sometimes poor families may not struggle to put food on the table, but this food may not be nutritious enough to provide the energy they need to work or to study. When prices rise, more and more people are affected.

IT'S A FACT

Rising prices have a greater impact on the poorest nations. People in low-income countries spend about two-thirds of their income on food, while those in high-income countries spend about a fifth, on average.

FOOD SUPPLIES

The food you buy in a supermarket has been on a long journey. It may have been grown overseas, processed elsewhere into the product you buy, then packaged and distributed. A disruption to any one of these stages can affect the whole supply chain, making food less available and more expensive.

Changing conditions

Every year, crop yields change. Temperatures and rainfall patterns affect the way crops grow, and climate change has made conditions more unpredictable. Pests and diseases can also have an impact on production. Farmers in high-income countries can use pesticides to maintain their crop yields, but lower-income nations can't always afford them. In times of conflict, disaster, or political change, there may be a shortage of labor and fewer seasonal workers to help with the harvest.

Temporary seasonal workers are hired to plant, harvest, and pack crops. During the Covid-19 pandemic, travel restrictions had a severe effect on the availability of this workforce.

Wasted food

In low-income countries, crops can be lost in the field to pests and diseases but 40 percent of food can also be lost in the supply chain, often due to inadequate transportation or storage conditions. If food is traveling long distances, packaging needs to keep it free from contamination and fresh enough to eat. In high-income countries, consumers tend to produce more food waste. In parts of Europe, for example, households generate over half of the total food waste – food that is bought but not eaten.

What Can I Do?

If you buy local food and seasonal produce, you're using a shorter supply chain, reducing energy use and the risk of food waste in transportation. Try to reduce food waste at home too. Plan ahead so you only buy what you need, store food safely, and check best-before dates.

Raw sugar is being loaded onto this cargo ship. About 80 percent of the world's population relies on imported food, but some countries, such as Canada, the United States, and Argentina, produce enough food if they wanted to be self-sufficient.

TACKLING FOOD WASTE

According to the Food and Agriculture Organization (FAO), about a third of the food we produce for humans to eat is lost or wasted each year. This makes it more difficult for us to feed a growing population, but it also has far-reaching consequences for the environment. Food waste accounts for about 10 percent of global greenhouse gas emissions.

Waste not, want not

When food is wasted, it also wastes the land, water, and energy used to produce it. Rotting food in landfills releases methane into the atmosphere too. Better packaging, storage, and transportation can help to avoid food spoilage in transit, but we can also make use of the food we throw away. Less than two percent of the valuable nutrients in food waste are currently recycled. These could be reused or reprocessed as animal feed, fertilizer, or textiles and other materials. We also need to embrace misshapen fruit and vegetables – a third of this "imperfect produce" is thrown away before it reaches supermarket shelves.

Local markets sell misshapen fruit and vegetables, but if there's demand for them in shops too, fewer stores will throw them away.

Efficient supplies

In recent years, technology has helped us to redistribute some of our food waste. Apps have been created to advertise unsold food from cafes, bakeries, and restaurants, to be sold at a fraction of the price. We can also be more conscious of our food choices. Meat, for example, is an energy-intensive food source. Farmers use a lot of land, water, animal feed, and energy to raise livestock, such as cows. Replacing some meat dishes with plant-based foods can help to lessen this impact.

What Can I Do?

Think about the types of food waste in your home and get creative with your cooking! Candied peel makes use of fruit skin, leftover stems can be used in soup, and overripe fruit can be blended to make a smoothie.

A third of our crops are fed to livestock, who eat more food than they produce.

FAMINE

In some parts of the world, extreme conditions can cause a large population to have inadequate access to food. We call this famine. People die from starvation, and malnutrition leaves others vulnerable to disease. In the 20th century, famine killed nearly 75 million people. Although statistics began to improve, climate change and conflict are raising the risk of famine again.

Combined causes

Famines are often triggered by a natural disaster, such as a lengthy drought, when water is scarce and crop yields fail. In recent years, climate change has increased drought conditions, particularly in sub-Saharan countries such as Kenya, South Sudan, and Somalia. Poverty and political situations can also make the problem worse. A country may experience extreme price increases (see page 8), or conflict may restrict imports. Sometimes, food can be used as a weapon of war, by cutting off supplies or humanitarian aid.

This is a dry river bed in Kenya, where years of insufficient rainfall have caused the worst drought in 40 years, destroying crops and making food scarce.

A woman carries her son as she waits at a food distribution center in Yemen. Civil war has affected food security in this already poor nation.

Rapid response

When a famine occurs, humanitarian organizations such as the World Food Program (see page 26), bring supplies to those in need and help communities rebuild their lives. Experience has shown that swift action is the key to survival. In 1985, the US Agency for International Development created a Famine Early Warning system to record and predict rainfall trends, price increases, and levels of agricultural production to help anticipate or even prevent future famines.

AVERTING DISASTER

In 2010–12, a devastating famine killed a quarter of a million people in Somalia. A severe drought caught many refugees as they fled the disruption of civil war, making them extremely vulnerable. Five years later, Somalia was on the brink of famine again, but this time international agencies were prepared. The Somalia Emergency Drought Response and Recovery Project addressed immediate concerns, as well as creating resilience for future shocks.

These refugees in Somalia are waiting for vital food aid to help them survive extreme drought conditions.

REGIONAL VARIANCE

Like poverty, food insecurity is a global problem, but some regions are particularly affected. Rapid population growth, climate change, and soil degradation can make matters much worse. In 2020, 54 percent of malnourished people lived in Asia, 36 percent lived in Africa, and about 7 percent lived in Latin America and the Caribbean.

Local problems

Two of the poorest regions of the world – sub-Saharan Africa and South Asia – are facing additional challenges. With its population expected to double by 2050, sub-Saharan Africa has had to rely on increasingly expensive food imports. South Asia currently has enough food for its population, although climate change will be a challenge for future crop yields. This region has high levels of malnutrition, however, because insufficient sanitation has brought a greater risk of infectious disease, affecting the body's ability to absorb vital nutrients.

This Guatemalan girl has been donated a meal at a malnutrition clinic. Around half of children in Guatemala are malnourished.

Unfair advantage

Many low-income countries rely on their agriculture as a source of income. But in a fiercely competitive world, the poorest nations often lose out. Farmers in high-income countries may be given subsidies (money) to increase production so that food prices stay low. When multinational companies employ cheap labor overseas to keep costs down, it's difficult for local farmers to compete with their prices. And if the companies buy or rent land to grow produce, local communities can't grow the crops they need to sell or to eat.

FINDING A BALANCE

After crop failures in 2022, India put a partial ban on wheat exports to keep local prices down and to ensure there was enough wheat for its citizens – a move we call "protectionism." The world was already short of wheat, due to weather conditions and the war in Ukraine, and India's actions caused a further increase in its global price. India was trying to find a balance between its role as a global wheat provider and a desire to protect its own markets. Some nations were exempt from the ban, however, such as Egypt (a country highly dependent on wheat imports), neighboring nations, and lower-income countries struggling with wheat supplies.

Crops grown to make eco-friendly fuels (biofuels) are big business. This valuable farmland in Brazil now grows two successive crops in a season – soya bean and corn – for the biofuels market.

THE RURAL-URBAN DIVIDE

Cities are thought to be richer than rural regions because they have more jobs and government investment, and a bigger selection of shops and restaurants gives greater access to food. Although rural areas are at more risk of deprivation, poverty exists in urban areas too, and not everyone in cities has access to a nutritious meal.

City struggles

In recent decades, China and India, the world's most populated countries, have seen rapid migration from rural to urban areas as people seek better livelihoods and lifestyles. In India, the infrastructure hasn't kept up with demand, causing city slums to develop. A household registration system in China has limited migration to urban areas, but slum-like villages have grown up on the outskirts of the cities.

Sleek skyscrapers are the backdrop to this slum area in Mumbai, India. The city's population has more than doubled since 1991.

Adapting to change

Urbanization takes over valuable farmland for building and development. As the land that's left becomes more valuable, farmers may be tempted to sell up and move on. Those who stay try to get the most out of their land, but this intensive farming can make the fields less fertile. One solution to support rapidly growing cities is urban agriculture. This can range from small community gardens and allotments to indoor vertical farms, cutting transportation costs, and shortening supply chains.

SINGAPORE'S CITY FARMS

Singapore is an Asian city-state with a completely urban population. Since the 1960s and 70s, Singapore has relied on its neighbors for food imports, making it vulnerable to disrupted supplies and price shocks. The government is now aiming to produce 30 percent of the nation's food locally by 2030 – using initiatives such as vertical farms and laboratory-grown meat.

Indoor vertical farms in Singapore are transforming food production. The farms need more energy for heating and lighting but save on water and transportation.

COSTS AND CONSEQUENCES

Poverty and food insecurity can create a vicious cycle. Poverty increases the risk of food insecurity, while in turn food insecurity can affect a person's health and well-being, reducing their ability to earn a decent living. As more and more people are affected, there are cost implications for governments and the global community too.

Hidden costs

The types of food you eat are important. If your body doesn't get the nutrients it needs, your general health can be affected. You may lack energy and your immune system can be weaker, making you more vulnerable to disease. Poor nutrition can also affect your sleep and mood, making it more difficult to study or to hold down a job. Countries bear the brunt of malnutrition, too. In the United States, for example, malnutrition costs the government about $3.5 trillion ($500 per person) each year, putting additional pressure on healthcare services.

Fast food is usually cheap and easy to access, but lacks nutritional value. In high-income countries, malnutrition can be caused by poor food choices and an unbalanced diet.

Social unrest

When food becomes scarce, the demand for fewer products causes prices to rise. But food scarcity can also cause social unrest. Many wars have traditionally been fought over resources, such as oil and land, and some people think future wars could be triggered by food insecurity and water shortages. In Sudan in the early 2000s, for example, competition for water and land triggered social unrest in the region. Recent years have also seen protests in Argentina, Indonesia, Greece, and Iran over price rises and food shortages.

In 2019, people took to the streets of Buenos Aires, Argentina, to protest against the government's economic policies, worsening conditions for the poor, and rising hunger.

What Can I Do?

It's easy to feel helpless in the face of global problems, but there are simple things we can all do to make a difference.

- Donate tinned and dried produce to food banks that help those in need.

- With the help of a parent or caregiver, volunteer to collect and distribute food donations from shops and restaurants.

- Sign a petition or write to your local representative about policy change (increasing the minimum wage, lowering the cost of nutritious food, or supporting fair trade policies – see page 29 – for example).

- With a parent or caregiver, get involved in a community garden or allotment to grow fruit and vegetables for local residents.

CARING FOR CROPS

Over the last century, we've lost 75 percent of our crop varieties in our desire for high crop yields and "perfect" produce. An estimated 40 percent of plant species are also at risk of extinction as we clear more land for farming or development, and feel the impact of climate change. To make our food supplies sustainable, we need to rethink how we farm.

Diversification

We're relying on too few nations for our food supplies, but we're also relying on too few varieties of produce. Over 75 percent of our food comes from just 12 plant and 5 animal species, but scientists believe we have around 200,000 edible plant species. By rotating crops, we can improve crop yields and soil conditions, and reduce the risk of pests and disease.

We could also use natural fertilizers to reduce the environmental impact of synthetic fertilizers, which are made from minerals and oil, release greenhouse gases when they're used or produced, and pollute the environment.

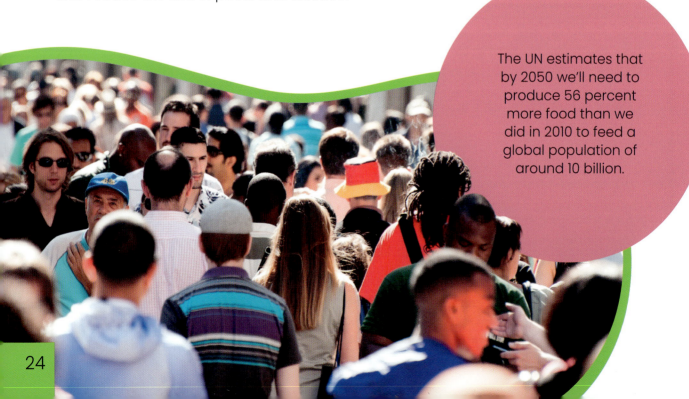

The UN estimates that by 2050 we'll need to produce 56 percent more food than we did in 2010 to feed a global population of around 10 billion.

Drones can be used to monitor soil conditions, to find diseased or damaged crops, and to spray fields with essential nutrients for a higher crop yield.

The power of tech

The modern world is often blamed for the difficulties we're facing, but it's also giving us answers and solutions. Technology, for example, can help us to make our farming practices more efficient so we get the very best from our land – robots, sensors, and drones can monitor and improve growing conditions; automatic planting, watering, and harvesting can reduce labor costs; and the use of data and artificial intelligence can help us to predict future conditions.

PLANTS FOR THE FUTURE

In 2008, a global seed bank was opened on the Norwegian island of Spitsbergen in the Arctic Ocean. Housed under a mountain, this facility stores over one million plant samples from nearly every country in the world. It's like a back-up drive to save our plants from extinction! There are now over 1,000 seed banks around the world. Some are used to cross-breed plant species, creating crops that produce higher, more nutritious yields that are able to withstand climate change.

Seeds at the Svalbard seed bank on Spitsbergen are stored at 0.4°F (−18°C). The Arctic conditions and thick rock ensure they remain frozen even if power is lost.

INTERNATIONAL COOPERATION

The modern world is increasingly connected, so it's important that we all work together to resolve global issues such as poverty and food insecurity. Groups such as the United Nations bring countries together to achieve more than they can alone. The World Trade Organization works to keep trade running smoothly and the World Bank and International Monetary Fund offer financial support.

Rice from the World Food Program is loaded onto a ship bound for African countries affected by an outbreak of the Ebola virus.

Key organizations

As part of the UN, the World Food Program is the world's largest humanitarian organization. It provides emergency food relief and works with vulnerable communities to improve food nutrition and sustainability, thanks to voluntary funding from over 60 governments. Also part of the UN, the International Labor Organization monitors working practices to ensure that conditions, hours, and wages in food production and farming are fair, while the World Trade Organization works alongside the UN to help governments negotiate trade agreements, to keep food imports and exports flowing freely.

Working together

Throughout the year, world leaders gather at summits and conferences to discuss key global issues, such as poverty, food security, and climate change. The UN's sustainable development goals (see page 5), for example, are monitored and new targets are set to keep things on track. Key parties with firsthand experience are also consulted, such as scientists, business leaders, farmers, environmental activists, and consumer groups.

IT'S A FACT

Since 1995, the UN has held an annual climate change conference, bringing world leaders together to discuss ways to fund and resolve growing climate concerns.

Governments rely on scientific data to plan climate policies. Ice cores can show us what Earth's atmosphere was like when snow fell in the past and how these conditions are changing.

A SUSTAINABLE FUTURE

As our population grows and our climate changes, we need to have a sustainable food supply that is accessible and affordable to all. It's not just about producing more food or having more money to buy it. It's about making ourselves more resilient to shocks and unexpected circumstances and addressing the root causes of poverty and food insecurity, as well as the immediate effects.

Swift action

Most countries agree that we need to tackle the underlying causes of poverty and food insecurity, such as inequality, education, and environmental protection, but it can take time to reach an agreement on what the priorities are.

While we work together on solutions, we need immediate humanitarian aid. We also need international negotiations so that conflicts don't disrupt supplies of key products, such as food, fuel, and fertilizer, and protectionism (see page 19) doesn't put lower-income countries at risk.

High-income countries fund additional humanitarian aid in times of crisis. Military aircraft carry loaded trucks to reach remote regions as quickly as possible.

Moving forward

Poverty and food insecurity are two of the world's biggest problems, but we're already well equipped to solve them. We have enough food to feed everyone, but we need to adapt to changing circumstances. We also need to grow more crop varieties and widen our source of suppliers, so we're more resilient to future shocks and crises.

We need to reduce barriers to education and employment, so that more people have access to nutritious meals. And lower-income nations need support so they can compete fairly on the world stage. It means making changes to our food habits, but if we all play our part now, small changes can add up to make a big difference.

What Can I Do?

When you shop for food, think about the impact of your choices. Where does your food come from? How much money, water, or land was needed to produce it? Consider buying fair trade goods that guarantee a price for farmers and help to supply fertilizers, pest control, and development in the region. You could also use customer feedback forms in stores to demand change.

This Kenyan woman harvests macadamia nuts as part of a fair trade program, helping to support development in the area.

29

GLOSSARY

biofuels Crops such as corn and grain, grown to make eco-friendly fuel.

conflict A serious disagreement between nations or groups, such as fighting a war.

Covid-19 pandemic An infectious disease that emerged in 2019 and spread around the world.

crop yield The amount of produce grown per unit area of land.

discrimination When someone is treated unfairly for being different because of their race, age, gender, or disability, for example.

economy The way a country or region spends and makes money.

exports Goods or services that a country sells to another country.

fair trade An arrangement that ensures fair prices and working conditions for producers in lower-income countries.

greenhouse gases Gases in Earth's atmosphere, such as carbon dioxide and methane, that trap heat and cause temperatures to rise.

humanitarian aid Emergency aid, such as food and health care, provided to a region in a time of crisis.

imports Goods or services that a country buys from another country.

infrastructure Transportation systems and communication networks, such as roads, railways, power supplies, and internet access.

malnutrition A lack of proper nutrition, leading to ill health. It may be caused by lack of access to nutritious food or the body being unable to absorb nutrients.

migration Moving from one place to another, such as from a rural to an urban area.

refugees People who have been forced to leave their home country because of war or disaster.

sanitation Facilities that keep a place clean and free from infection, such as access to clean drinking water and sewage disposal.

self-sufficient Being able to maintain one's needs, such as access to food, without external help.

slums Squalid and overcrowded urban areas with poor housing and sanitation.

soil degradation When soil loses its fertility because of overuse or environmental conditions.

spoilage When food or other perishable goods go rotten.

sub-Saharan Africa An area of Africa that lies south of the Sahara Desert.

subsidies Money given to an industry to help protect jobs and to keep the price of their products low.

supply chain The processes involved in the production and distribution of goods.

sustainable Able to continue over a long period of time.

United Nations An international organization founded in 1945. Its 193 member states work together to maintain international peace, security, and cooperation.

FURTHER INFORMATION

Books

Poverty and Hunger (Stand Against) by Alice Harman, Franklin Watts, 2020

Poverty and Our Future by Gene Brooks, PowerKids Press, 2022

The Poverty Problem by Rachael Morlock, Rosen Publishing, 2022

Websites

globalgoals.org/goals
Learn more about the UN's sustainable development goals.

worldslargestlesson.globalgoals.org
Fun activities and resources can help you make a difference.

dosomething.org/us/campaigns
Check out inspiring ideas to take action in your community.

INDEX